WHEN I WAS A POET

WHEN I WAS A POET

DAVID MELTZER

The Pocket Poets Series : Number 60

City Lights Books | San Francisco

Library of Congress Cataloging-in-Publication Data
Meltzer, David.
When I was a poet / David Meltzer.
    p. cm. — (Pocket poets ; 60)
 ISBN 978-0-87286-516-7
1. Meltzer, David—Poetry. I. Title.
 PS3563.E45W47 2011
 811'.54—dc22
                                    2011010348

City Lights Books are published at the City Lights Bookstore,
261 Columbus Avenue, San Francisco, CA 94133.

Visit our website: www.citylights.com

CONTENTS

PART I   WHEN I WAS A POET *9*

PART II   AUTOBIOGRAPHIES *23*
Cold *25*
"It's me at 12 or 13" *34*
Mr. Peanut *38*
Doom Cusp *47*
California Dreamin *51*
All the Saying Said *55*

PART III   FRENCH BROOM *59*

PART IV   LEMME BE: AMULETS *69*
Protection *71*
Abstain *72*
Amulet for Silence *73*
Night *74*
Wing Amulet *75*
Typewriter Amulet *76*
Amulet for Song *77*
Ibbur Amulet *78*

PART V   POEMS 79

"It gets down to the basic way" *81*

"I return from a past that never entered
    itself" *82*

"Broke the wing's edge over my head, that" *83*

"Cupped, Tarzan yodeled. . . ." *84*

"asking questions leads to more" *85*

Hello Death *86*

"God fuck the loss that" *87*

"& then we vanish to become the book" *88*

"All the dead" *90*

Dreams *91*

"in the dark we park our sharks" *94*

"supreme ream" *95*

"lovers go wherever they can" *97*

11:9:01 *98*

"16 viii 97 Nusrat Fateh Ali Khan" *99*

Pepper *100*

"in the passage" *102*

"Found this in the whirlpool:" *103*

A Slew of Blues *104*

Jewelbox *107*

Zone *116*

PART VI   DOG THE LION *119*

Night Reals *121*
Dogma *126*
David Dog the Lion *136*

PART I

When I Was a Poet

When I was a Poet
I had no doubt
knew the Ins & Outs of
All & Everything
lettered
in-worded
each syllable
seed stuck to
a letter
formed a word
a world

When I was a Poet
the World was
a cluster of Words
splattered upon white space

When I was a Poet
I knew even what I didn't

I thought I knew the Game
whereas the Game knew me
played me like an ocarina

When I was a Poet
I was an Acrobat
a Tightrope Walker
keeping balance
in my slippers
on a wire above
Grand Canyon
Inferno
Vertigo

Oh I did prance
the death-defying dance
whereas now
death defines each second
of awaking

When I was a Poet
everyone I knew
were Poets too
& we'd gather at spots

Poets & Others
met at & yes
questions yes
w/out pause
w/ no Answer

Ultimates
certainly
Absolutes
absolutely
but otherwise
Nada
Zilch
great Empty
blank page
blank stare
into the core of it All

When I was a Poet
Willie Nelson
was back to back w/
Paul Celan
side by side
on the Trail of Tears

no worries
no Gravity
wide eyes awake
zeroing into
all edges
& lights of the ordinary
extraordinary

Fools for Love
Fools for Freedom
dance as mites & fleas
into the Void
worldless & wordless
my red diapers
gird me

When I was a Poet
aloof & above
free of Doubt
a Chopper view
encompasses grand
Map of the spread
of what's to know

hit the streets
from bar to bar
stooling Truth
to cadres
compatriots
jot dots
connecting All
together
as we've always known
Everything to Be

When I was a Poet
Everything was Possible
there wasn't Anything
that wasn't Poetry

Voyant supreme
skateboarding Void
no fear of falling
even when falling

When I was a Poet
Passion was a Wire
plugged into Nerve Ends

of lover Spines
charging our volts
with Jolts of Jazz
& deep juice
parting like Red Seas

dig It
Creeley said

When I was a Poet
knowing It
within Measure
& Beyond
free-falling
re-forming
riffing
24/7

disconnected
from Jack's "electrics"
getting It all down
on paper w/ pen
pencil or typewriter

watching paper stack up
towers of profound
poetry Babel

When I was a Poet
Death was a metaphor
a traditional glyphic
rampant metaphysic
Immortality assured

while Dante's midway
or Coney's boardwalk
spilled over
& vanishing became routine
& all of the hummingbirds
who darted in & out of each line
got grounded

When I was a Poet
Everything was a Revelation
no Detail less than Cosmic

When I was a Poet
Eden dew
made my raiments
soggy

Nectar got me groggy
but Visions woke me up
Battle of the Bands
& Bonds
wdn't let me off Easy
despite the Breezy gab
sprung forth from
Clucked tongue
in yr Ear sworl
yr Labial lips
me burrowing
deeper & deeper into
Within's heat
slick slippery perfume

When I was a Poet
I Grieved & Raged
against Now & Then & Knew

it was all about Letters
shape-shifting into Words
& Poems that cd salve & solve
most Grievances
even Death's Silence

When I was a Poet
I knew Nothing
& Everything
& now
I'm in between
the lines
signs everywhere

When I was a Poet
no need to know it

Each word the word
revealing the word
I cd trace it like shooting stars

Each letter luminous
& liminal

& auratic w/ shimmer
to put them together
in the flow of flux was deluxe
swam in it
the light made seeing possible

When I was a poet
poetry was all there was
each beloved exalted
beyond the margins

everything & nothing was
poetry to me
all I could see & be
was poetry
heaven everyday
all the way down to
my grungy socks
up to my ozone wisdom
know zone

When I was a poet
it all made sense as

poetry in motion ongoing
forever & ever

Now at the end of the line
the letters assigned as words
sound out in brain's dome

When I was a poet
was a thief, a jackdaw
of all traits, straight
to the shining things

Jongleur, juggler
fast footed rollerskater
in rinks & poetry halls
swimming in yodel wobble
stretched tape of extreme waltzes
& blotched blue spots
turning ice into ink

When I was a poet
everything was Poetry
hummingbird & maggots hatching

Everything & nothing counted
all plugged into Heart Central

.

PART II

Autobiographies

COLD

1.

Heat of freeze
glare of
her blue eyes
ice picks

2.

Rimbaud was heat
despite
icy blue eyes

3.

Bowers of icicles
hung from each word

Shards of ice
slice transparent wounds
exposed flesh

4.

She never was anything less than
camera ready

5.

To the end spoke in a little girl's
high pitched sing song voice
insouciant but insistent

6.

All clothing
form fitting
absolutely crisp
neatly ironed
regalia to support
orange pancaked fratz
& terminally bleached hair

7.

Iron freeze, her
razorblade spine

8.

How she multiplies
into a cardealer spread
of faces

9.

Who knew or knows
why or when she stopped
playing the Wurlitzer harp
exiled in the Brooklyn garage
the Steinway baby grand
in the living room she
like an anorexic picked at
but no longer played

10.

her hot boney flanks
ass side against my
kid plump heat

11.

bear the wrist scars
of Rockville Center

12.

with all her extravagant
boxes of Charms
chewing gum
furs & musk
a moviestar mom
visiting me in
camp death watch

13.

flat glamour of suburbs
diningroom wall mirrored
rec room basement w/ faux wood
paneling, well stocked bar
TV, new furniture in living room
protected by plastic rubbers

14.

Nailpolish deep red
Plymouth convertible
her ice blue eyes
behind the wheel

15.

Dry ice demon
inexplicable
its damage
its immense heat

16.

How blue eyes
signify ice
& dark eyes
the schmaltz

17.

Her Auschwitz body
w/ blue eyes & blonde
hair in Brooklyn shtetl

18.

Torment
torn between
& in between
dark heat
& cold doubt

19.

An L.A. harpist prodigy
chunky dimpled
in publicity photos
rejected her body
shrunk it into survivor
pancake makeup
skeleton serving food to
Jewish aunts & uncles
cousins & brothers of
her husband's clan
which he accepted
as she repudiated

20.

she had a plan
a way out & back
into harp-filled path
of Looney Tunes
sincere rapture
& class elevator ascension

she had a plan
deeply unknown
until the time
it opened its
lotus
to focus
on escape

21.

we kids don't know
her mystery
remains & retains its
disinterest

22.

Nan & I
talk of numb
long distance
wires of
she says
I say
we all say

Pops was hot
Mom cold

23.

back to the ice of her eyes

•

It's me at 12 or 13
at the Royal Roost w/
Pops digging Bebop
& his chubby kid
drifting on a reed

Speed Graphic $1 shot
the leggy babe w/ a tray
of smokes snaps two
generations together
because of the music

My dad a mystery
more approachable
than mom the blue
heat of ice in our lives

Brown eyed sorrow
big laugh pies in the mug
knocks the trance into dance

•

Am serious but
want to make people laugh
I'm my father's son

Am serious but
a tummler
my father's son

Am nearly 3 decades
older than my father
when he died

My father's only son
in our struggle to be the same
yet different
yet the same

My mother's only son
in our struggle to be close
became more apart

My mother & father's progeny
3 daughters, 1 son
was raised in a female sphere
round orb of womb

Never learned what I know
yet knew it before I could
read each letter of the alphabet

Was too young
to be so old
& now too old to be
so young yet
bones & sinew
bid adieux

One never
gets to
the end of it
as if the beginning
was clear & certain

So wrapped
enraptured by

closures & openings
my father's son
held his hand down streets
even as a teenager

•

MR. PEANUT

These shards, shells, splinters & glints
for Michael McClure—Arf!

Mr. Peanut
a guy inside
a peanut shell suit
w/ tophat & cane

stands in front of the Broadway
Planter's Peanut Store
hawking
hot peanuts inside
fresh peanut brittle
waves his cane in mystic loops
his voice works up circles
through a monocle

•

sometimes
there'd be two
Mr. Peanuts outside

lacquered into
Mr. Peanut shell suits

smell of goobers roasting
in sputnik vats
whose perfume's fingers
drew you to the counter

●

$^1/_4$ of a pound for a quarter
filled you up for day
couldn't keep away

food for thought
for keeps

before anything
Mr. Peanut

●

Mr. Peanut looked at me
out of a shell

through zero
a monocle

Blind beggar w/ dog & accordion
a few feet away plays
Sempre Fidelis

Democratic
down to earth
Mr. Bee Nut
Be nut. Bee nuit.
Lord & Lady Peanut
sovereign goobers
who ariseth from
the southern earth
as Osiris

•

Brought big bags to the Ritchers
& we got stoned & watched TV
w/ sound turned off
listening to LPs of Al Cohn &

Zoot Sims
dueting

gravel of peanut meat
scrape down grass-dried throats

•

As a kid I ate hot peanuts
shell & all & said
the best flavor was in the shell

•

My grandfather revealed
a prophet concealed
in every peanut split in half

•

Moondog: Mr. Peanut

•

slots in his shell
secret compartments
like Batman's utility belt
the symmetry
fascinated me

•

talk of "making yr nut"
leads to concept of concealment
(shelled), of unity

"I made my nut;
I got it made"

•

Mind shifts to shell-game

under a half-shell
a seed's moved around
through sphere to sphere

the game's managed by an operator
Mr. Peanut's shelled & w/in him
a seed whose energy is shelled
& this shelled energy
enters into the mandorla
into constantly
shifting spheres until
it all coheres

．

breaking out: prison: shell
break into: bank: shell
break through: satori: shell
break-down: satori: shell

．

speak thru husks of shells past
snail leaves its shell behind
snake leaves shed form on the road
what's left behind is
journey's history
already losing clarity of detail

•

of course the products that march us
soldiers thru neon banks of plastic
stuff spastics: buy buy buy buy
Mr. Peanut pencils sweatshirts cups dolls

•

Mr. Peanut as Fred Astaire
debonair savoir fair

•

it's easy to write "Bolinas" poems but
standing in front of Planter's Peanuts
in front of the masked Mr. Peanut on
Broadway right next door
to the RKO Palace where Judy Garland
(who isn't Billie Holiday)
another story altogether

•

Okay. Where do broken shells
of all those peanuts go?
Out the window
onto the ground
to mulch
fuel for California poppies.
Too much mulch the Pharaoh says
cleaning his teeth w/ headlines
impersonal death's compressed into.

·

shell game out of Barclay's
back from Grand Central
gotta grab a cab to Ballantine

·

NYC/1968: Tina's hand in mine
walk quickly up from Avenue of Americas to
Broadway

in a hurry
where are we going?
you'll see

44th and Broadway
after 22 years

•

25¢ bag of hot goobers
shared w/ Tina
this feast of poetry
& poverty's nutmeats

•

DOOM CUSP

In Memory of Wallace Berman

Munir Bashir's 'ud alone
in his Baghdad studio
1987

"Music is one
We're all human beings
The same family
Music is for everybody"

The past that won't
catch up to
the present

History makes itself up
until others
make it up

"acute homesickness"
Greek: *nostos*
"return home"

algos "pain"
Nostalgia

The retrospectives
catalogs of old photos
of young lovelies

ME: "harm, oppress"
Old French, *grever*
"to burden, encumber"
ME: "hardship, hurt, sorrow"
grief/grieve

Burden of past
Weight breaks
Down early grace of
Supple unknowing

Grow to know
Death's musk
On the cusp

Edge of Chrysler
Deco edge

film loop
Eternity
freezes

Stuffed w/ death
a glut knish
unable to wish
before or beyond

Mourning is memory
a "Withering away"
as if there's a choice

Greaves
death's dog food
also
bait for fish remove

Worm into words which
Wallace the bookworm
warned me against

Am in the ozone
no zone liminal

fat w/ past
bogged down
in the tense present

Sink in drink
expand & shrink
(spine) gone

detoured to there
where nobody's here
unless they're dead

almost there

•

CALIFORNIA DREAMIN

California dreamin
schemin in a doorway
to get more pay when none's around
the corner panhandlers come up short

Gold Eden jackels prowl & Jack
London stands on a burning deck
socialism sinks on clotty city blocks
indigent exiles from the good life
last month last week
can't last too long on TV hallelujah
chorus cigarette smoke Night Train
billboards above streets slapped on walls

California dreamin
in Brian's garage
Sunkist shades slow glow
amble down buckling pier
meet oceans halfway in Nikes
telephone psychics at castle switchboards
hello Cosmos give me Doctor Presto

California dreamin
next door to Anita O'Day
in a white one-piece swimsuit
under multi primary color umbrella
smoking a cigarette
tapping high heels

California dreamin
Lord Buckley on stage raging
crossover baptism crooning
hipness & apocalypse
stoners swoon in midnight balcony
after crummy print of Top Hat

California dreamin
highnoon blaze junkie flash
orange grove bonkers fat green
leaves filter light on outstretched hand
stings with citrus acid watch
veins move blood through the system

California dreamin
Utopia's just around the corner

lodged beneath overpass freeway
teaching mimosa Off Minor changes
jazz livingroom altar the new Miles
crash on carpet Bye Bye Blackbird
TV's soundless plush glimmer
Ronnie Ball's wife rolls up in delight
red bulb lamp Dear Old Stockholm
ah oh Coltrane

California dreamin
schemin steamy encounter
w/ two guys & one
Breck girl airline stewardess
blonde all the way in lipstick
golden sheen uphill breasts nipples
tough as rubber to tripletonguing
trumpet player chops chomp
later on top of Sunset sex w/ a pro
doing it for fun all night long her
tough toned flanks take me everywhere
later ass grabbed in Troubador Club
in music stream of dancing bodies warm
light scrotum radiance alert

California dreamin
Hollywood Boulevard occult bookshop
tower to ceiling shelves of glyphed tomes
brittle dreambooks powdery gold pages
copper scrolls scratched w/ sigils
promise of future power triumph
watching Pacific Ocean waves weave in & out
thrum shore we sit in profound bud
wasted on gravity & detail
all of us artists rising above the
weight of things

•

ALL THE SAYING SAID

roar of webwork branching w/in
metastasizes
despite the light between us
what's to be said
blood clouds swell & cast out
vast inescapable traps
body economy's energy
focused on each remaining moment
what anything means or meant
gets lost beyond belief
it's time to change the bag
plugged into your neck
whose fluid nourishes
life against the death
it also nourishes

we've been together
so much of our lives
now dying unties that
willing weave
we are preoccupied

w/ matters too large
too small & adhere to
medicine's time tables
liquid morphine every half hour
change Fentanyl patch every three
run down stairs for ice
chunks to suck on
shark cartilage enema
Amanda lifts you out of our bed
to the commode
edema swells your lean legs
cancer weeps rusty oceans
your belly distends
pregnant w/ death

what's to be said
what's unsaid
no banter
no word play
no more singing
you can barely speak
& then it's basics like
"water" or "more morphine"
a dream so precise

in each second's unfold
nobody could believe
all that did & didn't happen
all the saying said

•

PART III

French Broom

Allow me these fragments
They are my poem
My poem is pieces
Here & there
Chips off the old blockhead
One wall cracks apart
Not from despair but rain
Plaster falls on the floor
Reminds me of a poem
I write whenever I get
Time to sit down.

•

Others balance by
Kneeling to pray
I allow them their poem
This is mine
A patchwork poem
Pathwork
Dream flesh sewn to
Flesh of wounds whose edges
Cut against the mouth
Don't turn away.
My blood mixes with plaster
Sealing the poem together.

•

One letter, one word
One line at a time
Held in the page
When I sew pieces together
They remain fragments.

Typewriter strikes paper
Needle thru cloth
Allow it.
My grandmother was a seamstress
My grandfather a tailor
My father sat before his table
Sewing jokes into the air
Something like satori
To think of it
Splinters my brain.
No judgment
Let me be with my pieces
Spread upon my table

•

A puzzle no matter
How I move it
Never solves itself.

•

Time unbends me
My fragments make no difference
They are children
Laughing against knowledge
Shadows grow large in the field
My window watches
Sunset swallow song
Stars arise
Page after page of my book
Writes thru time
Lights sewn together
My poem is bits & splinters
Darkness allows me.

•

Into dawn
The door opens.
Quail in pairs
Wobble out for seed
Scattered like stars
In random swirls around the green
Grace of bamboo
Moving supple in the wind.

•

Question my poem
For words to describe it
The page is in pieces
Praises, sorrows, joys
Corny sincere
Spirals of aura dust
Fragments & whispers
Thumb book of holy hints
All are my poem
& they bend to a moment
Ready for distraction

•

Breeze
White clouds
Blue sky
Yellow buds
French broom
Opening.

•

PART IV

Lemme Be: Amulets

PROTECTION

I have 10 faces on both hands
I spring at you
Whenever your back is turned.

•

ABSTAIN

Abstain.
An amulet for the harp.
The 10 stringed harp.
Play it only before sunrise.
The rest of the day declines into wine.
Trust song that comes from a cup.

•

AMULET FOR SILENCE

Unplug the world.
If that's too hard,
turn off the electricity powering your house.

.

NIGHT

Keep night company.
Sing to her as she turns the pages.
The better your song the more lovely the light
She offers in return.
It is not a contest.
It is a binding.
A singing together.

•

WING AMULET

SO I MAY FLY FASTER THAN DARKNESS
KEEPS BACKING ME AGAINST A WALL
I CAN NO LONGER VANISH.

•

Wing me above so below is a painting.

Paint me with wings, a helicopter above the bench
chops rolls of paper into books.
Wind from my wings turns each page
my black sweat splatters text in space.
Open the book and it turns into wings.

•

Against the King of nightfalling without stars or hope
Against the King of nightfalling swallowing dreams
Sucks death from our mouths before we can sing
This amulet wants wings to work against the King
    of nightfalling.

•

TYPEWRITER AMULET

Be reinforced against poetry's fists.

Cement its four poles to a firm base set beneath the great fig tree. Under heaven song shall be pulled from its rollers.

Scroll sheets hot off the branches cut into tabloid by sun spokes.

Protect each key.

Praises.

•

AMULET FOR SONG

About your place go swallowing stars.

Grab them off branches. Wear asbestos gloves.

Husk stars correctly, with care. Place them upon well-tilled soil. They sink into earth and become white stones you weigh and wear in a band above your elbow.

Whenever darkness returns, you need not worry.

Now you may stay there and write and sing and read mystery books to yourself or anyone else who can break through the vision surrounding your place.

•

IBBUR AMULET

Invoke you out to see if there's shape beyond imagination.

Invoke you out to see you invoke me out.

All on a screen watched by others turning inside-out, looking to see if there's a shape beyond imagination.

.

PART V

Poems

It gets down to the basic way
we/I/you live, die
Do life,
know death. The rest
is restless.
Lots of mirror
lots of terror
lots of rare
unknown complaints

•

I return from a past that never entered itself
on a page or in a museum
a memory one among ten whisper
bowing at light's edge.
Whatever I do never finds face in a book.
Assembling words already caught
is to knit barbed-wire crowns.
Hunt the escaped song
without technology, not inside
typewriters. Enter this white room
to see me type without paper.
Touching the past
beyond those words sustaining me.
Remainder and skeleton of my soul
lice to remind of laughter.
Limit of mastery not transcended.
Tell me if my touch is gentle
or prolific in its blindness.

•

Broke the wing's edge over my head, that
tablet of fire I called angel.
I saw it in my words, saw its wings move
and was content with its metals, felt
protected by its spine. Once
named itself Vav, 3rd letter of the 4 letter
Name, blessed our home, table, bed,
the desk I work on. Vav
first seen in a phonebooth on Masonic.
Vision requires love's attention but I
push against the edge of romance spreading
over my head and my bed fills darkness with ink.
Memory tram
slams out all
glass windows.
Snowfall splinters
turn into blood,
the poem angels sing, arising.

•

Cupped, Tarzan yodeled for a herd of elephants to decimate the white hunters drilling for oil in the heart of his jungle.

They capped him king. Forever captured on the screen Tarzan will never be free to sing with power again. Who hears him sing immediately giggles or squirms about in discomfort. He is now a cliché where before he was a warrior and singer without peer. This is history.

•

asking questions leads to more
questions requests quests for not
necessarily answers or doors opening
into floors where truth should be just
around the corner bright-eyed & fanged
it's a thankless task

•

HELLO DEATH

hello death hovering around Tina
her shrunk face severe angular
ivory luminous parchment powder
coats her skin her belly's Rwanda
distended sips on strawberry kefir
thinned w/ low-fat yogurt
we apologize for distance
stuck in our distinct pain chains
we still want to chitchat the everyday
binds & holds our rite together
a hummable tune art rides on

•

God fuck the loss that
leads me downward
not even in enjoyable spirals
instead dense dumb blank erase

Whose face there
immediate & above?
Present but past.

So much confession
too much mea
too much culpa
too much
who gives a fuck
about losing a life
& gaining a faith?

•

& then we vanish to become the book
which is our tomb

& then we vanish not within but beyond
all those photographs others remember
time with

the "we" is of course me

here in *Ragas* typeface

here sensing Death
the send of seeing
the book the page
the letter the word

easy enough
"tomb" & "womb"
no immortal
needs the Ouija
for that ah ha

clotted by layers
of wrong fuel & foods
building death within

yes, death
yes, da'ath
yes, the dot that
hits center
to unfold
& explode

•

All the dead
the living
the in between
always here
& malleable as skin
in time's impress
knowing everything
knowing nothing
praying & preying
we stay until we leave
& those who grieve
mourn themselves

•

DREAMS

The watch whose hands fall off. Tina giving me
the what's up with yr life? look & then we dance
smoothly into each other. Too briefly.

●

Tina's naked back my hands my fingertips reach
out to touch the heat.

●

Tina's naked back suddenly available to my touch
before the phone rings with the wrong number.

●

Eating an olive filled with forgiveness.

●

Buying you a bird which refuses to fly or speak
and in fast-motion decays and dies and is a tiny
pyramid of muddy feathers.

•

The glisten applied to your eyelids.

•

Shekinah is wingless and is cleaning wineglasses
from the night before with a soap that smells of
mulched roses.

•

How many more years to undream?

•

How to re-dream?

•

Embers of your heat are mirages like steam I reach for before they turn into cold awakening.

•

in the dark we park our sharks
in the shark we feed our ark
in the ark we're stark raving
in the end we're not friends
in the end we can't bend out or up
instead we mend & watch our ways
pray for souls already lulled
into piety stupor which is pity
which is terror to be stuck
face to face by death's mystery
death's mastery

•

supreme ream
dreams of fluid drive
keeps pricks alive
in twangy red heat

beat your meat you
dismal twit you
shitfaced dimbulb
stuck on hold

all this gargle of God
lightenment
tenement of broken parts

homeless hearts
out on a looksee
for ecstasy
a popper you
chopper your
brain with O
pisspot

what you got
another day duller
& deeper in rot

•

lovers go wherever they can
to love & kiss in doorways
on steps leading into houses
they might someday live in
expect no reason
it's mating season
they move on to other
protected spots
down the block entwined
look into each other's faces eyes
see only love

•

11:9:01

sketchy sleep then
early morning voice mail
have you heard the news
Gloria says
I'm not crossing over the bridge

Aya wants to know the exact time
the first hijacked plane hit the tower
eastern standard
since she was psychically
plugged into it all

& in TV's false river of light
reminds me how it was
prophesized a decade ago by
metaphysicians
& the mothership
hovers above us ready to land

•

16 viii 97 Nusrat Fateh Ali Khan
dies in London age 49
last bliss devotion grain flake
drops into maya's
fallopian tube
recircles anew into
larger Bally Sagoo Rumi
qawalli worn out cassettes
cabbies play in & out flak of
dispatcher directives

•

Nusrat dead at 49 died in London
overweight & light as Allah's
99 Names emanate from One
to One

•

PEPPER

Art's desire to get it all said
to all who thought him dead
in the joint & beside the point

Art's struggle to sing it all
through jazz warfare & tell
everything he knew in brass
speed rap stir crazy utopia
of muscle chops push it in your face
rough unrelenting grace

fierce Art pitbull clamps down
pulls edges out in time to break through
scream knotty beauty
toe to toe w/ any joe
who thinks they know better

Art tattoos blue needles into moonlight skin
junk light makes mirrors perfect

Art's smoke aches out of wounds

L.A. Art burritos & bebop
black guacamole serge zoots
Central Avenue cat copping

Pepper at Club Alabam
in Lee Young's band
all the chicks & the hatcheck chick
have big eyes for Art's horn

•

in the passage
way away from
sea, the light
takes hold of all
hands can touch
& toss as bombs
into the dark
ahead & behind

●

Found this in the whirlpool:

To see us then
resistant &
glamorously young
now dead or dying

to see is not to be
to be is not to see

to know
is another problem
altogether

•

A SLEW OF BLUES

heaven when it happens
is another closed door
you wait behind
going blind
w/ smashed cup
jammed into your hand
& nothing to do
but sing the blues
to all the other ones

•

dark eyes
white thighs
quiet nights
soft guitars
broken jaw
detached retina
looking for love
in all the wrong places

•

how low can you go
how deep is the ocean
how low is down
how high is up
drink the moon from a tin cup
crow sun to sons & daughters
sleeping at the torment wheel
drive everywhere nowhere

•

Once it was the lost road
now a thread of red
vein weave crashing out
shuts down the system
step by step
loss by loss the great cosmic imaginary
literally shuts down
& whatever's there
vanishes, is gone

•

I can't last much longer
I feel like I'm going down slow
below the low
beneath the bottom
bottoming out into new
levels of flop
new gutters soft & spongy
inhaling my draggy bones deeper
into the outside
whose toxins feast
on meat's fact & renders all
into beginning all over again

anonymity
no more anything
fingerprints
iris corona wide
blink in flash

I'd be rich like Rockefeller
if you belonged to me

•

JEWELBOX

for Julie Rogers

the love that loops
around yr spine
at touch
rewinds its electricity
surrounds our bodies

no touch simple
lit nerve filaments
connect to core

no kiss simple
to tender wet lips
connected to core

nothing simple
then again
nothing complex
connect to core
shuffle disappearing words
up to the ceiling

•

loop of longing
a lasso around your naked body
shine sweetly on our bed
drenched in love sweat
slipping & sliding thru
infinity w/ the greatest
of ease reborn
what else is there to know?

•

delights in the dark
smudged by candles
hint at curves of
naked open beings
we're so busy
entering into &
being entered
eyes shut
eyes open
seeing what can't be
be

•

a-mazing
a rose garland
wraps around us
in deep sex perfume

look
listen
forget
remember

it's gathering first thoughts
first deep embrace
deep release
open realization

so much more
beyond plans or
certainty, as
easy as peeing
as singing

just clearing my throat

•

big gift of beginning
wide scope
big picture
small detail
little mole
remarkable

•

newborns in a playpen
laughing & throwing
kaka at each other

•

sing of the joy
my mouth finds
in yr armpit

•

almost full moon

fat & shiny
startled me
pouring a glass of water
from the kitchen sink

.

freeways of old ways
marshmallow collapse
in sci-fi melt

where are we going?
why do we hold hands?
kiss at red lights?

call me tomorrow

.

if there were walls
soft as our bodies
I'd be bouncing off them
24/7

•

sweet sweat slick
laminates our flesh
open window breeze
goosebump legions
as we invade deeper heat
surrender willingly to the salt

wet glisten of
your diamond face of
facets

my nervous tongue
moves towards
yr pink lights

•

in repose
spread out on unmade bed
white curves of yr body
ever surprising continent

•

fingertip delicately
stroking yr wet lips
before a deep kiss

•

love so hidden
wound w/in like
a rubberband ball
bursts its bonds

love aloft
flying
over damaged maps
dead river scars burning

hit dry ice clouds
cherub-shaped
spin out into
bowls of melted chocolate
where I see you
your soul

emerging out
towards me

soar away & towards
seek nest
seek home
to root & rise
in sun & luna
brief eternity

•

if we are
wild animals
tearing into each other
intent to ravish
w/ joy & pleasure

then let's stay
in our forest
start a bonfire around
our tangled bodies
that refuses to be extinguished

•

tongues touch beyond mind
yet write the writhing
afterwards

•

ZONE

poems are
unsaid
not said

they can be anything
from shopping lists
to legal briefs

but it's what's not there
that's there

nothing to do w/
everything

always something
elusive

words work best when
they know they can't

nothing changes
but vocabulary

•

PART VI

Dog the Lion

NIGHT REALS

1.

Night when it's light placed on paper,
tracked-down. Dear lights
haunt me. I seek it in black.
Her round hills still give me thrills.
Song against dark. O mere words.
Mother tongue furl to scoop tar out of milk.
Endless possible sea.

2.

Night the canopy our poem shapes.
Bend over song.
Pull long veils down majestic hallways
or stalled on a Freeway to stammer
ultimate truth. Any moment.
Night the canopy blesses bent-over peon
tills royal soil of invented earth.

3.

Night fights like no other.
Brother against brother.
Sanctioned by Gillette Blue Blades.
Sectioned flesh looks back through blood mouths.
His tongue knots against left-hook.
Hits the deck. Out. Jake
Lamotta's blond wife in a white suit
splashed with blood Sugar Ray
slams out of Jake's face.

4.

Night space,
a closet to cry in.
Fur and cloth veils.
Muffled wailing.
Pain condensed,
I plant it within.
A coin deep inside
dark overcoat pockets.

5.

Night races,
a dream. Dawn scythe
doesn't hack my throat.
Alive with song,
I drive starlight
over paper.

Arise, touch eyes open
to read notes of poems
left over from dreams.
Bones cold.

6.

No father no mother
I'm an orphan
No father no mother
I'm a stranger
No father no mother
An exile

No father no mother
No sister no brother

Let me stay with you a while.

7.

My father died before I was 22
in the first year of my marriage.
My mother invented death an amulet
against the ghost of my father
peering through her kitchen window.

In the mirror, day after day,
my skin darkens into night.

8.

You look back where once fearful shadows stalked
and see the sea, a shadow in the mind,
move beneath moonlight.
Letters, numbers, codes
lead to nothing.
Stand up and curse it.

Damned thing in the blood.
A molecule. Fool's drool
strings out until it snaps.

Down to the shore for more roaring into waves
which are cities to break hearts into portions,
fragments broken off a sun.
You look backwards or forwards
yet words stop, run-down.
Who is left to speak to and what do you say?

Dawn loon skims over the lagoon in silhouette,
sings a crazed song, unable
to tame my rage into haiku.

•

DOGMA

Many years I have travelled
I travelled far enough to know
You can't find no heaven
Nowhere in the world you go.
Henry Townsend: She's Got a Mean Disposition

And who cares
    Not shaman bears nor Chinese root-men
instead old oak mudra
    flashed and panned off sunset.
All of it a glove.

    Enter triumphing
o'er sage plains. An act of eye
    level lines, pen blacks on blue note
books. Confines. Digs. Sublime
    an active word dog-eared in all
editions, additions
    to ripe bulk of type
bending rude wood shelving
    exposing short parchment crotches
silk ribbons tying ancient skins
    together, as if from them
a golem will be re-circled into being.

Parchment-yellow shadows.
     Granpa Granpa.
Hillfolk handling candles.
     Reel after reel.
Broke telephone lines snake
     spark up against unfounded ground.
America already behind the others on line.
     Ellis Island
morphing-up language.
     My pedigree Mongol Slavic
Lithuanian Polish. Uncle
     Jess in Minneapolis writes
"the family name's another story,"
     but not Meltzer which bankteller tells me
means "waiter" in Hebrew. Snap snap!
     Haifa cafe. Hey, waiter,
bring me another anisette and I
     stooped and masked, assume a Buddha
nistar Galli-Galli, proffer mystery bottle
     to he who waits, who breathes in circles,
slow clouds of inwardness.

Shaman pissing power into earth
Shaman sucking marrow from bones
    for neck rattle
Shaman stacks spine discs on pole so recordplayer
    flips them over easy and chant after chant
    slits the parade of hits into blood soup drunk
    afterwards for courage.

Mongol mutt poets cure as well as cause disease.

    Medicine being as it is
keeps life or takes it
    out of gravity
flatly pressed into amulet for survivor.

    Little turtle
squat on bottle cut
    over nose bridge
drummed-out pain despite blood rain tattoos
    in galaxies on shaman's tomtom.

Hatchet mouth wide.
    Ascetic shaman, cryptic.

Rattles teeth,
    gourds the knot,
trances fancy, traces it
    to heaven or hell
on a thread of saliva easily looped
    from victim's coma.

D Mutt the Mongol Tartar Cavalier slave to
    justice, goodtimes, the flowering cunt.
A mouth, a triad, flat slap of Tarot icon on
    formica or ancestor oak. Eyes spare nothing
nada. Tongue gulps out its catch in symphonies
    misrepresented by teletype or telestar
questar satellites up there
    gobbling more light.

D Mutt the Mongol mongrel King's soldier cross-
    bearing the sixpoint star of David mugged
flypaper zipped-up, not to be trusted.
    Nectar sipped through hot-mouth ocean.
Trumpet valves pushed down. Lightning bolt.
    Let's face the beard in all her
    in all his

in all them
in this and that vocabulary of reunion.
No more setting apart what wants in.

Not Marcel's R Mutt or Nutt but D Mutt,
    dog-headed being, his master's voice, a mongrel
filed, de-briefed and burgered who bog-trots forth
    kennel poems with deft con's paws, shapes
sawdust into bibles into biscuits for the trickster.

    Lineage lost. A stain on lambskin.
Dog's angel name erased. Forever hang-dog.
    Upside down hungman. Licks alert
red clay parts into more dog-kids.
    Mongol clods, shamans and tailors,
humping and bumping up and down all over the
                                        world.
    Each mutt is D Mutt, not Jeff's Mutt, not
Mutter earth birth-clap in space. Before that
    starlight, dog sparks
        looking for a home.

Paper dog not paper tiger out of
    putsch pain. Arfans and orphics
lap-up clouds.

Paper dog tower of bark
    outruffing stark low-cut street rut.
Mono-cult junk riff. Remember
    seed your cans with garbage.

    Back from Mongol stir-fried shoots and pods
and hot-sour soup, adam's apple awake
    with white pepper and chili oil
braised tofu sauced with ginger, scallions, all of it
    bathed in R Mondavi bulk magnum Chablis.
Who is he, this maitre de
    so nonchalant and Waltly sauntering
from wok to soup pot to Arrowhead peanut oil
    bubbling forth of soysauce and ginger and roger
it's over before you scorch flamenco fingertips.
    Hiss of kickedback oil when shoots and
                                        snowpeas
hit the sauce and mushrooms splatter the air
    with indelible pain rubbed out with sesame oil

on meat of thumb and left hand palm.
    Understand?
This is how D Mutt the poet hashes out
    the history of food.

•

D MUTT BIOGRAF FRAGMENT
    (Transcribed from the tape):
Entering into/onto 4th Tree:
    3 mothers/daughters aspiring to stardom,
a son not yet a year but still lionic Adam and still
    near the freeway sea yet now removed
to a longer room. White-walled the will still
    pushes back into black Hebrew wallscape.
Scrape glaze off skull. Laser clay
    off soul. Breath in a bottle.
Parent as well as ventriloquist; conjurer
    Davies notes in Celtic-Hebrew scholarships.
Yet another brotherhooded Eden O David
    hey Abrahama supremo snake and Egypt
sizzling red smoldering typeface of Nile's edge.
    Dark red clay, the stuff, held up on firstborn's

                      day

to offer myth new light. To touch upon the 4th
    Tree's 10 wicks topped with Tarot discs in
assorted occult kabbalistic colors. Crayola angels
    dab eyebrows and mouths in harmony
with charlatan harlots. Still open. Hot acceptance.
    Dance to read prose or poesy or see poses
on postcards. British Museum: Rosetta Stone, 5 p.
    That coded block part of the clutter
the matter of history, an endless accumulation.
    Sorcerer's apprentice madness. Artifacts and
paper stacks balloon and multiply at full moon
    and D Mutt, demented, joins wolfmenschen
and luftmenschen on line. Hunger haunted words.
    Hunt them in libraries. I have trusted
their shapes too long. A scriptic dance conveying
    all the possible poses of mystery. And poetry
broken into sends alarms out the tower but
    type-night breaks no sky nor stops hearts.
Dead trees collapse upon each other
    thin skins black with language.

....

History mysterium play misty for me
    on my knees in data dust. Must be shaman
mongol of Russian four-bears on hind legs,
    winged, chains drag against nettled flank.
Naked shaman beings travel in air
    on curled clouds on oceans of magic
weather reports, current events. Chthonic
    numinous demonic zeppelins ever upward.
Then backward for the word-cure.
    Psycho-bio escalator. Beginnings.
Art the mark pocked off that first ritual sickness
    thick in clotting streams. Depth-charge knots.
Wrassle snakes O help spirits
    any chance you have, swaying and spirited
through it all. I am life-line
    and in my brought-back words
the life you hold onto. In trust
    I am on a journey for your soul.
Old grandma Mongolian cheekbones.
    Yellow scrollskin. Thick black hair.
Cataracted eyes. Eurasian Grandpa.
    How far back before first snake egg?
Out popped the shaman link
    whose poetry is to be always back and forth

but never fully welcome in one's hut
    unless sickness invades order
and in chaos is shaman summoned to make right.
    Alright. To make it well, to bind it back again
as it was without him. His presence menacing.
    His art a necessity.

·

Jew dog howls amulet clouds.
Hemah, a death angel, approaches
on tip-toes like a dancer.
Cloud lace of garlic fails.
God's dog not a dragon.
Perhaps tomorrow.

·

DAVID DOG THE LION

David Dog the Lion
bounds across Brooklyn
like a greyhound & monkey
coils around the streetcar
going to the Subway
there's a War going on
he paws it all down at the Rugby

David Dog the Lion
rollerskates through Brooklyn
WW2 BMT to Coney Island
roller racketing on Boardwalk wood
ocean unfolding onto shores
Luna Park on the other side
big smile of Tilyou you cd get
sucked into as into a big fish
David Dog the Lion the Monkey
scrambling through cotton candy
Nathan's hot dogs jiving &
thriving & dare you to catch me
on the boogie boardwalk

over the fence onto the sand
facing the ocean opening its brine
for an epic swim to California

David Dog the Lion unreal eel
sliming down Hollywood Boulevard
stalks stars with true unagi pizzazz
gets snagged by PR paparazzi
put on public access TV
need an agent to fend off offers
in those hyper moments
before the right one snakes
into the cacophony realism
of fake moments glass shards
piercing eyes & told as history
bleeds from tight lips
mute as memory evaporates
each second it's received

David Dog
in Lion country
can't afford to
tread lightly
nor love unconditionally

really lost in between camp
fires & shadows of others
who may be Lions
aligned in packs
like we used to do
before fire

David Dog
the Lion looping
loping over evaporating
habitats makes eye contact
w/ Polar Bears swimming into
certain starvation

David Dog from the start
knew a thing or two
but then forgot
foraged like a skinny rat
through the mountains
pyramids of shiest shit crap
unused uselessness
as a native in those cities
he was after all a New Yorker

David Dog the Lion
lost & found
red prong sprung out
plugging & unplugging
sometimes stuck in
heat holes along the road

David Dog the Lion
driven by certainty
so fractured
it's kaleidoscopic
musky inside doghouse
uncertainty melts the leash
at last & again I'm off

David Dog the Lion
the once-upon-a-time lemming
chases cats & squirrels
but not racoons
they're way too tough
for this soft heart barker
sometimes doubts his own bark
his weave of woofs

a furry aria
no one knows what to do with

Ariel mutt angel David Dog
bounds down the hill too fast
buckles to his knees
tearing fur & skin
sad sack mutt crumpled beneath
giant redwoods

David the Dog the Lion
wonders about his progeny displaced
all over the place

Postscriptum

Wonder about "dog" his name
celebrated mystery words
of English etymology
recorded 1st in 1050
probably born before then

dogs & gods
guardians

David Dog the Lion
straight out of Brooklyn
now on the run from
Dog Catcher gods on speed
w/ GPS tracking my pawful flight
into awful laser lights
O DDL known for
fidelity nobility
keeper of boundaries
between this world
& the next
guardian of the passage
guardian of the underworld
skid around cement corner
rip a hunk of hide off
my bony body

David Dog
the Lion Buddha
companion of the Mother Goddess
of all huntresses
fire bringer

hits the dirt scrambling
away from AK 47 bullets
hey
I thought this was the US of A

David Dog the Lion
lost in the bullet holes
like starry scars

lights out
for now

•

Copyright © 2011 by Steven C. Wilson

Born in 1937, David Meltzer is a poet associated with both the Beat Generation and the San Francisco Renaissance. He was also included in Don Allen's seminal anthology, *The New American Poetry 1945-1960*. A child prodigy, Meltzer performed on radio and TV in New York beginning in the late '40s. In 1957, after a few years in Los Angeles, where he was part of the circle around Wallace Berman's *Semina* magazine, Meltzer moved to San Francisco, where he associated with such poets as Allen Ginsberg, Robert Duncan, and Jack Spicer. One of the pioneers of jazz poetry readings, Meltzer also formed a psychedelic folk-rock group called Serpent Power with his late wife Tina and poet Clark Coolidge, recording for Vanguard Records in the late '60s. In addition to his many books of poetry, Meltzer also published 10 erotic novels in the late '60s and early '70s, including the critically acclaimed *Agency Trilogy*, revisiting the genre in 1995 with *Under*. He has edited many anthologies, including the book of interviews, *San Francisco Beat: Talking with the Poets* (City Lights, 2001). He also taught for many years in the poetics program at New College of California. In 2005, Penguin Books published *David's Copy: The Selected Poems of David Meltzer*. Lawrence Ferlinghetti has called him "one of the greats of post-World-War-Two San Francisco poets and musicians."